Life's a

PUPPY
PARTY

Life's a PUPPY PARTY

Recipes, DIYs, and Activities for Celebrating the Seasons with Your Dog

HEATHER HUNT

Photographs by
JOSH BLANEY

Vet's Note by
DR. SARAH MACHELL

TILLER PRESS

New York London Toronto Sydney New Delhi

An Imprint of Simon & Schuster, Inc.
1230 Avenue of the Americas
New York, NY 10020

First Tiller Press hardcover edition October 2021

TILLER PRESS and colophon are registered trademarks of Simon & Schuster, Inc.

For information about special discounts for bulk purchases, please contact Simon & Schuster
Special Sales at 1-866-506-1949 or business@simonandschuster.com.

The Simon & Schuster Speakers Bureau can bring authors to your live event. For more information
or to book an event, contact the Simon & Schuster Speakers Bureau at 1-866-248-3049 or
visit our website at www.simonspeakers.com.

Interior design by Jennifer Chung

Manufactured in the United States of America

1   3   5   7   9   10   8   6   4   2

Library of Congress Cataloging-in-Publication Data

Names: Hunt, Heather N., 1988– author.
Title: Life's a puppy party : recipes, DIYs, and activities for celebrating the seasons with your dog /
by Heather Hunt ; photographs by Josh Blaney. Description: New York : Tiller Press, 2021. | Includes index.
Identifiers: LCCN 2021011759 (print) | LCCN 2021011760 (ebook) | ISBN 9781982167554 (hardcover) |
ISBN 9781982167561 (ebook) Subjects: LCSH: Dogs—Equipment and supplies. | Dogs—Food—Recipes. |
Handicraft. | Do-it-yourself work. Classification: LCC SF427.15 .H86 2021 (print) |
LCC SF427.15 (ebook) | DDC 636.7—dc23

LC record available at https://lccn.loc.gov/2021011759
LC ebook record available at https://lccn.loc.gov/2021011760

ISBN 978-1-9821-6755-4
ISBN 978-1-9821-6756-1 (ebook)

Illustration credits: Home and Pencil by Alice Design from the Noun Project;
Safety and Bone by Adrien Coquet from the Noun Project; Parasol by b farias from the Noun Project;
Flower by kirana from the Noun Project; Maple Leaf by fauzan akbar from the Noun Project;
Christmas Snowflake by ProSymbols from the Noun Project; Paw by Fithratul Hafizd from the Noun Project;
Think by Mello from the Noun Project; Exclamation Mark by TMD from the Noun Project;
Party Hat by Fabiana Antonioli from the Noun Project; and Star by lauriel from the Noun Project.

For my mom:

Thanks for teaching
me that even the
smallest celebrations
deserve a party.

CONTENTS

INTRODUCTION

In the summer of 2016, I had zero children and zero plans to have children, but I was reading parenting blogs for eight hours a day.

My job in marketing at a New York City children's clothing start-up meant that I spent all day every day immersed in content from the internet's most popular parents—their favorite snack recipes, colorful DIYs, themed party ideas, and seasonal shopping guides.

Being a mom was far from my mind, but my husband and I *were* spending our nights obsessively researching puppy adoption. The day we brought home Dave, our tiny and neurotic four-pound dachshund puppy, was one of the best of my life.

As a newly obsessed pup parent, I was ready to go all out on celebrating life with our little guy. I wanted to bake him dog treats and throw him a half-birthday party and sew him a Halloween costume. But I had no idea which ingredients were safe or how to plan a puppy party or where to shop for dog clothes. I assumed that a quick internet search would serve up the kind of modern, high-quality blogs that I was used to reading for work. And sure, there were plenty of online resources for vaccination schedules, diet information, and training programs, but the fun stuff? Not so much.

Almost exactly a year after Dave joined our family, we brought home a corgi named Elizabeth and launched TheDapple.com, the kind of fun and modern pup-parenting guide that we felt was missing online—a place where you could read about rescue organizations but also find instructions for throwing your dog a Harry Potter–themed birthday party.

In the three-plus years since then, we've been overwhelmed by the reception to our site. We never imagined that we'd get so many emails from dog owners who had been looking for a blog like ours, or that we'd get to attend VIP events where people wanted to tell us how we'd inspired them to plan their pup a barkday party. We've loved every minute of learning, growing, and celebrating pup parenthood with our readers.

When the kind and enthusiastic team at Tiller Press/Simon & Schuster approached me about developing a pup-parenting book based on our blog, it was just two weeks before most of the US would go into lockdown for the COVID-19 pandemic. After an initial conversation that ended with everyone on the call excited about the project, I assumed the book would be cancelled because, well, who was really feeling like celebrating anything in March 2020?

After my editor reassured me that the book was still happening, I spent a lot of time trying to sort through my own feelings about creating something so small and silly at a time dominated by so much sadness. And as I did, I kept coming back to all the conversations (and DMs and emails) that I've shared with our readers over the last three years. For so many of us, it's the little silly moments that make life with a dog especially beautiful and joyful, like watching their excitement over a new toy or a playdate with an old friend.

With that in mind, we've created the book that we wished was available when our dogs first joined our family—a guidebook to celebrating life with your dog all year long. We've included over forty recipes, DIYs, and activities that can be adjusted to work for dogs of almost any size and breed. And just to make sure everything will be fun and safe for both you and your pup, all activities and recipes in this book have been reviewed by Dr. Sarah Machell. Dr. Sarah is a veterinarian with over two decades of experience in small-animal veterinary practice, a dog mom to three very adored pups, and the medical director of Vetster.com.

We're so honored to share *Life's a Puppy Party* with you, and we hope it inspires you to have fun, make some memories, and celebrate each new year with your dog.

—*Heather*

A NOTE on YOUR DOG'S COMFORT and WELL-BEING from DR. SARAH MACHELL

What Heather has put together in this book for us dog lovers—to have fun and safe activities and joyful celebrations with our beloved companions—is just fantastic, and I was so excited to have the opportunity to review all of the activities and recipes! Keep in mind as you navigate all this fun that, just like us, all dogs are different—they have different needs, preferences, allergies, sensitivities, and emotional baggage.

Although I have approved the recipes and activities in this book, and we have provided you a few points to be mindful of along the way, know that they still may not be appropriate for all dogs. During any activity, always monitor your dog for signs of anxiety, avoid activities that cause them stress, and never leave them unattended with any of the costumes, activities, or ideas in this book.

Similarly, always consult your own veterinarian before adding new foods to your dog's diet. Many dogs have allergies or sensitivities to certain foods, and the recipes in this book may not be aligned with your long-term health goals for your dog.

Always research new ingredients before adding them to your dog's diet. The American Kennel Club's website (www.akc.org) is a great place to start when searching for pup-safe fruits and vegetables. While there are lots of human favorites that dogs can safely enjoy, many dog owners may not be familiar with the potential that foods like avocados and grapes have for toxicity in dogs.

Similarly, the artificial sweetener xylitol is often found in many human foods and is highly toxic for dogs. Many of the recipes in this book call for peanut butter, yogurt, or gelatin, all of which can contain xylitol. When cooking for your dog, always check the label and use plain and unsweetened gelatin and yogurt, as well as a xylitol-free, all-natural peanut butter.

Finally, consider using a lactose-free yogurt in recipes that call for yogurt. Most dogs do not produce the enzyme required to digest lactose and are therefore inherently lactose intolerant. Some can experience GI side effects as a result.

Be safe and have fun!

—Dr. Sarah

A FEW BASICS YOU'LL NEED

When Dave joined our family and I began to search the internet for dog recipes and DIYs, every idea I found seemed to call for woodworking tools, sewing machines, or specialty foods—deal breakers for our tiny budget and even tinier New York apartment. For that reason, we've tried to keep the recipes and crafts in this book as simple as possible—no table saws needed! That said, there are a few basics that will come in handy over and over in the different recipes and DIYs:

For Crafting

Scissors

Hot glue gun

Pen or pencil

Paintbrush

Ruler

For Cooking

Blender and food processor

Bowls (large, small, glass)

All-natural cooking spray

Aluminum foil

Parchment paper

Wax paper

Baking sheet

Microwave

Oven

Refrigerator and freezer

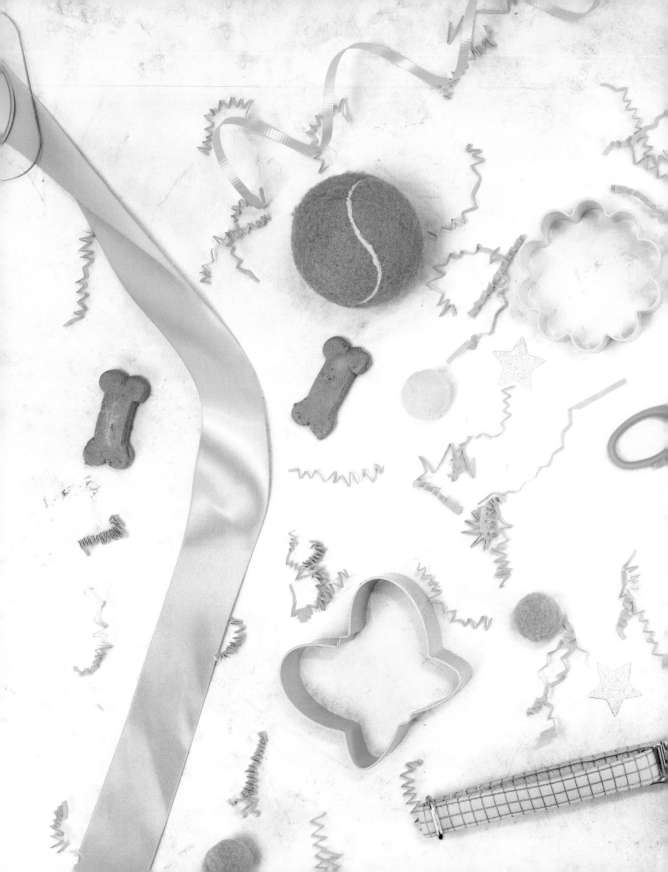

SPRING

✸

For dog owners, spring can feel like it's day after day of muddy paws and that inevitable wet-dog smell. But it's also a time to celebrate the beginning of warmer, longer days and the return of outdoor fun. In this section, we've gathered some of our favorite DIYs and easy recipes for making the most of this special time of year.

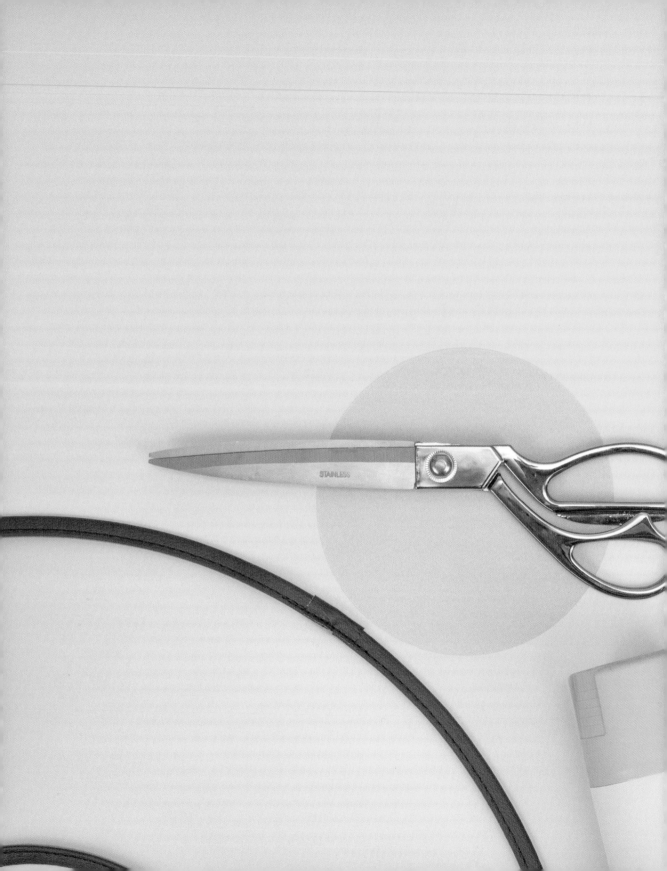

How to Turn a Medical Cone into a Spring Flower Costume

If your dog has been spayed or neutered, you probably have an old medical cone (aka the cone of shame) floating around your house. Instead of tossing it in the trash after your pup no longer needs it, give it a good ole glow up with this fun and easy hack that turns it into a cute spring costume.

What to Do:

1. Lay the medical cone flat. If your cone has a band along the outer ring, trim it off.
2. Take your round or heart-shaped object and place it on the flat cone. Trace around your chosen shape to create five or more flower petals. Some items that work well for tracing are a heart-shaped card, a roll of packing tape, or a vase. Cut each section into a petal by trimming along the lines you just traced.
3. Take the trimmed cone outdoors or into a well-ventilated area and spray paint. Depending on your brand, it may need more than one coat.
4. Allow to dry completely before using.

🏠 *Apartment-Friendly Hack*

If you don't have a good space to spray paint in, you can cover the cone with the heart-shaped note cards (the ones that you used to trace the petals) or colorful Post-its. Just trim the cone down and then hot glue the cards into place.

🐾 Don't forget—once you alter your pup's cone, it should no longer be used for any medical purposes.

You'll Need:

- 1 plastic pet medical cone
- Round or heart-shaped object (for tracing petals)
- Spray paint
- Hot glue gun (optional)
- Post-it Notes (optional)

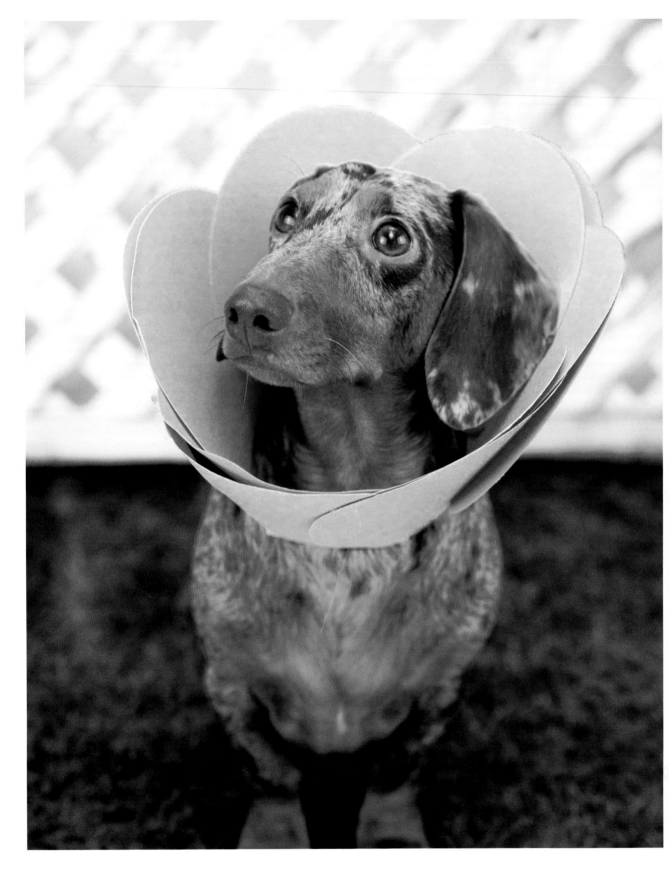

Spring Pom Bandana

You'll Need:

- 1 square white felt, approximately 10 inches
- Ribbon, approximately 20 inches long
- Hot glue gun
- 5 to 15 small boiled-wool pastel poms

In my opinion, poms make just about any clothing item better. Maybe that's why I love this simple and sweet wool pom bandana for spring. Between the poms and the bright pastels, it looks cheerful on even the rainiest spring days.

What to Do:

1. Trim a sheet of white felt into a square. For a medium-sized dog, a 10-inch square should work well, but size up or down as needed.
2. Fold your square diagonally and glue the ribbon inside, along the fold. Leave about 10 inches of ribbon on each side so you can tie the bandana around your dog's neck. You may need more or less than 10 inches depending on the size of your dog.
3. Cut wool poms into halves so one side of the pom is flat. Glue the poms into place, flat side down, on one side of your bandana.

🐾 Be sure to use boiled wool poms rather than classic crafting poms, since boiled wool poms will maintain their shape when trimmed down.

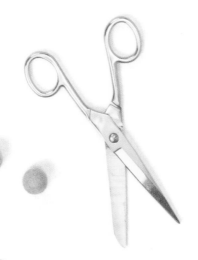

Spring Flowers Pupsicles

Raise your hand if your dog eats their treats so fast that they barely chew. *Raises hand.* We love to share popsicles with our dogs because it slows them down a bit and lets them enjoy their special snacks for longer. Plus, there are so many adorable ways to make dog-friendly pupsicles. I love this easy treat for spring that uses a tray of silicone flower molds to make beautiful, one-of-a-kind spring popsicles—just combine different pup-safe fruits for a variety of colors.

You'll Need:

- Fresh fruit
- Plain and unsweetened nonfat yogurt
- Silicone mold in flower shapes
- Popsicle sticks

What to Do:

1. In a blender, puree fruit and yogurt together. We recommend using a variety of fruit to get different colored mixes. Here are some of our favorite combinations:
    - Bright Pink: 1 cup frozen strawberries + ½ cup yogurt
    - Light Peach: 1 cup peaches + ½ cup yogurt
    - Dark Pink: 1 cup raspberries + ½ cup water + 1 tablespoon yogurt
    - Dark Purple: 1 cup blueberries + ½ cup water
2. Pour into silicone mold.
3. Lay a popsicle stick in each flower shape and freeze overnight on a flat surface.
4. Hold on to the popsicle stick and let your dog lick the sweet treat.

🐾 You can get a silicone flower mold at most craft stores or online retailers.

♥ *Safety First*

Remember that some fruits, like grapes and cherries, can be toxic for dogs. When in doubt, visit the American Kennel Club's website, which is a great resource for pet owners. And don't forget that treats with popsicle sticks included should only be shared while you're holding on to the stick to avoid having your pup accidentally swallow wood.

Easter Bunny Ears Costume

You'll Need:

- 1 standard wooden mixing spoon
- White cardstock
- Spool of half-inch-wide elastic band for sewing
- Hot glue gun
- Mod Podge
- White glitter
- Pink glitter foam sheet

Who knew a wooden spoon was the secret to creating an adorable pair of bunny ears for dogs? Well, we did, but only after a whole lot of trial and error. It can be tough to create bunny ears that will stay upright on a dog's head, but these little ones do the trick. And since they're not too big or too uncomfortable, your dog might even sit still long enough to let you snap a pic of the cuteness.

What to Do:

1. Lay the wooden mixing spoon on cardstock and trace its outline. Repeat a second time and then cut out your two spoon outlines.
2. Crease each cardstock spoon outline at the base of the cut-out spoon's bowl.
3. Measure how much sewing elastic you'll need for your dog's bunny ears by running the elastic under their chin and over the top of their head in front of their ears. You'll want enough elastic that the band will be snug, but not uncomfortably tight. When you've taken your measurement, add a half inch of extra elastic and then cut.
4. Lay your two cardstock spoon cutouts side by side on a table so that the bowl of each spoon cutout is flat and the handle sticks up into the air at a 90-degree angle.
5. Hot glue the sewing elastic right at the creases of the two spoons on the handle side of each crease, then hot glue and fold the handle of the spoon back across the elastic. At the crease, fold again and then hot glue the handle all the way up the back of each bunny ear to stabilize it on your dog's head. Trim the excess away.
6. Flip the bunny ears over. On the side that doesn't have the handle glued onto it, spread Mod Podge and then sprinkle with glitter. Allow to dry and then repeat so the glitter is thick and layered. Add a final layer of Mod Podge to lock in the glitter.

7. While the Mod Podge is drying, cut out two small ovals from the pink glitter foam sheet and set aside.

8. Once the Mod Podge has dried, glue the pink foam ovals onto the glittered side of the bunny ears.

9. Use the extra half inch to overlap the ends of the elastic and hot glue them together so that the band is now a loop.

10. Try it on your dog!

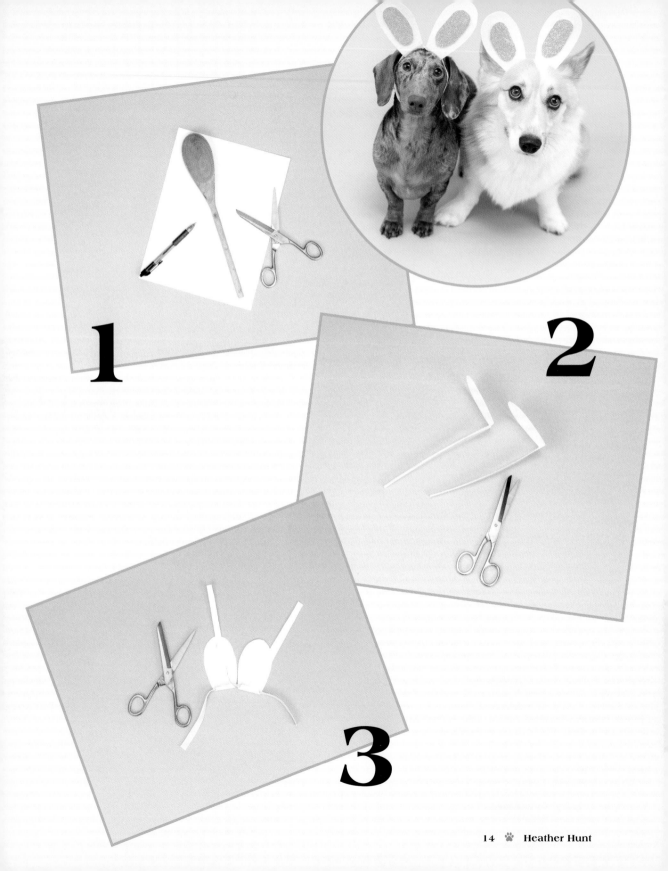

1

2

3

4

5

Not-Chocolate Easter Bunny

Most people know that chocolate is poisonous for dogs, but carob chips—which have a similar look and feel—are a fun and nutritious treat. If you're feeling like going the extra mile and making your pup their own Easter basket, one of these cuties is the perfect addition for any lucky dog.

You'll Need:

- Unsweetened carob chips
- Bunny candy mold

What to Do:

1. Eyeball the amount of carob chips that you think will fill your specific bunny mold. Then, in a small glass mixing bowl, microwave the chips in ten-second intervals, stirring repeatedly until the mix is smooth.
2. Spread the melted mixture into a bunny candy mold and freeze for about one hour or until the carob sets.
3. Remove and enjoy with your dog!

🐾 Bunny candy molds are easy to find at most craft stores or online retailers.

Vet's Note

Monitor your dog's reaction if this is their first time eating carob chips, since for some dogs large amounts of carob can have a laxative effect.

How to Create an Easy Easter Photo Backdrop

You'll Need:

- 70 to 80 plastic Easter eggs
- 1 large trifold poster board
- Hot glue gun
- Sticky Putty (optional)

Get that perfect Easter photo of your pup—and their friends!—with this easy and festive backdrop. Those good old trifold poster boards that you probably haven't thought about since the seventh-grade science fair make a perfect photo backdrop for your pup.

What to Do:

1. Hot glue the eggs across the trifold poster board in a random pattern.
2. Snap photos of your dog in front of your backdrop! Extra credit if you add the bunny ears from p. 12.

🐾 You don't need a professional lighting set for your photos to look great, but make sure that you set up the poster board in good natural light. For the best photo results, avoid direct sunlight or shadows.

🐾 *Think Big*

If you're trying to capture a pic of dogs who are too big to fit in front of poster board, it can be easier to use a white wall with good natural lighting as a backdrop. Just swap the hot glue for some Sticky Putty and decorate the wall for your photo background instead. And as an added bonus, it'll give you space to set the camera timer and get in on the fun!

Carrot Cake Doughnuts
for National Doughnut Day

Makes ten small doughnuts.

Did you know that the first Friday in June is always National Doughnut Day? It's the perfect excuse to whip up these tasty and nutritious carrot cake doughnuts for your pup. This recipe is full of healthy, dog-friendly ingredients like carrots and bananas, and it honestly just looks pretty darn cute. You might even be tempted to keep these in rotation way past National Doughnut Day.

What to Do:

1. Preheat oven to 350°F. Spray the doughnut pan with all-natural cooking spray.
2. In a small mixing bowl, whisk together the flour and baking soda. Set aside.
3. In a blender, puree the banana and oats until they create a smooth and sticky dough.
4. Remove the puree from the blender and place in a large mixing bowl. Stir in the egg, coconut oil, and applesauce.
5. Slowly mix in the dry ingredients and then fold in the shredded carrots.
6. Fill the doughnut molds ¾ full and bake for 12 to 15 minutes.
7. Allow the doughnuts to cool in the pan, then move to a cooling rack.
8. While they're on the cooling rack, sift yogurt powder over your doughnuts for a fun finish reminiscent of powdered doughnuts.

You'll Need:

- Small doughnut pan
- 1 cup whole wheat flour
- 1 teaspoon baking soda
- 1 large ripe banana, peeled
- 1 cup whole oats
- 1 large egg
- 1 tablespoon coconut oil, melted
- ½ cup unsweetened all-natural applesauce
- Small handful of shredded carrots
- Yogurt powder (optional)

SUMMER

It's hard to argue that there's a better time to be a pup parent than summer. The sunny days and long daylight hours are perfect for dog-friendly outdoor activities. From pool parties to popsicles, we're so excited to share a few of our dogs' favorite recipes and activities for staying cool and having fun in the summer months.

Puppy School Grad Cap

You'll Need:

- 1 paper baking cup
- Black spray paint
- 1 square black stiff felt, approximately 3 inches
- Small tassel
- Hot glue gun
- Spool of half-inch-wide elastic sewing band

The moment that Dave got his little puppy-kindergarten diploma was a proud one in my life. Not just because we had worried he was going to flunk—even back then he listened to commands pretty selectively—but because it felt like a sign that we were full-fledged dog owners. This DIY is an easy way to celebrate your little graduate and get the graduation picture I know you're dying to take.

What to Do:

1. In a well-ventilated area, spray paint your baking cup black. After thoroughly spray-painting, allow to dry for 24 hours.
2. Once the paint has dried, take the square of stiff felt and poke a hole in the middle. Pull the end of the tassel through it. Use a bit of hot glue to secure it in place.
3. Trim your baking cup down until it's roughly 1 inch deep. Glue the bottom to the side of the felt that doesn't have the tassel.
4. Eyeball how much sewing elastic you'll need to keep the cap on your dog's head. It should be just enough to attach to one side of the grad cap and then run down in front of your dog's ear, under their chin, and then back up to the other side of the grad cap in front of the other ear. It should be snug, but not tight. Cut the sewing elastic to that size and then glue each end of the elastic onto the sides of your grad cap.
5. Turn on some "Pomp and Circumstance" and get a pic of your little grad!

Pawtriotic Summer Bandana

You'll Need:

- Dark wash denim jeans (pants with a wide leg work best)
- White acrylic paint
- Plastic lid
- Star-shaped cookie cutter
- Dog collar
- Hot glue gun

I love a good upcycling project, and this patriotic denim bandana really delivers. The best part is that you can leverage the existing seams in a pair of jeans, so you don't have to sew. You'll just want to make sure that you have a jeans leg that's wide enough to make a bandana—something that will vary depending on the size of your dog.

What to Do:

1. Cut off the leg from a pair of wide-leg jeans, just below the knee.
2. Make a diagonal cut from where the hem and inside seam meet to the outside seam, about 10 inches up the leg. Then trim down along the side of the exterior seam, being careful to keep the seam of the jeans in the triangle of your design. You'll be left with a triangle that has two hemmed sides and one unhemmed side.
3. Pour a few tablespoons of white acrylic paint into a wide plastic lid that you no longer need. (I like to use one from a yogurt tub.)
4. Dip a star cookie cutter into the paint and then give it a little shake to remove excess paint. Stamp it onto the bandana. Cover the denim bandana with star prints and then allow the paint to fully dry.
5. Fold the unhemmed side of the finished bandana over an old dog collar and hot glue it into place.

Fourth *of* July Rocket Pops

Makes 2 rocket pops.

For me, rocket pops will always be one of those classic summer-time treats. When I look at them, I can almost hear the music from our neighborhood ice-cream truck. Here, I'm reliving those memories with this simple recipe that's made to be shared with your pup. The ingredients are favorites of both dogs and humans, and the instructions call for just enough berries and yogurt that you can make one pop for you and one for your dog. It's all you need for a perfect summer evening.

What to Do:

1. Thaw one cup of frozen strawberries and then blend with ¼ cup of water until the mix is a smooth puree. Pour into mason jars until they are roughly ⅓ full. Place in the freezer and leave for 1 hour.

2. Whisk the yogurt with ¼ cup water until the mix is smooth and milky. Remove the jars from the freezer and add the yogurt mix on top of the frozen strawberry layer until the jar is ⅔ full. Place in the freezer for another hour.

3. Blend the blackberries with ¼ cup of water until the mix is smooth. Remove the jars from the freezer and pour blackberry mix on top.

4. Cover the mouth of the jar with aluminum foil and poke a hole for the popsicle stick (this helps to keep the stick upright until the blackberries freeze). Place in the freezer and let freeze for at least 2 hours or until frozen solid.

5. Remove frozen popsicles from their jars by running hot water on the outside of the jar to loosen. Once removed, enjoy with your pup!

❀ Sharing Is Caring

Remember that treats containing popsicle sticks should only be shared with your pup while you're holding on to the stick to avoid their accidentally swallowing the wood.

You'll Need:

- 1 cup frozen strawberries
- ¾ cups water, divided
- 2 small mason jars
- ½ cup plain and unsweetened nonfat yogurt
- 1 cup frozen blackberries
- Popsicle sticks

Summer Gelatin Shapes

You'll Need:

- 4 cups of water, divided
- 4 packets of plain unsweetened gelatin (make sure it is free of xylitol)
- Beet juice
- Cookie cutters

Did anyone else make gelatin shapes in grade school? Although the fruity and sugary boxed mixes that you probably associate with gelatin shapes can be toxic for dogs, this easy recipe swaps out the bad stuff for a fun and healthy treat. This recipe is adapted from Knox Gelatine's classic Knox Blox recipe.

What to Do:

1. Bring 3½ cups of water to a boil. Meanwhile, sprinkle all the packets of plain unsweetened gelatin in a large bowl and pour the remaining ½ cup of water over the top.
2. When the water is boiling, stir in a few drops of beet juice until the mixture reaches your desired color. A word to the wise: a drop or two of beet juice goes a long way.
3. Pour the boiling mix into the bowl with the gelatin and stir until the gelatin has completely dissolved.
4. Pour the mixture into an 8 x 8-inch pan and chill overnight.
5. After the gelatin has set, remove from the refrigerator and cut into the shapes of your choice using cookie cutters. Keep refrigerated until your dog is ready to eat.

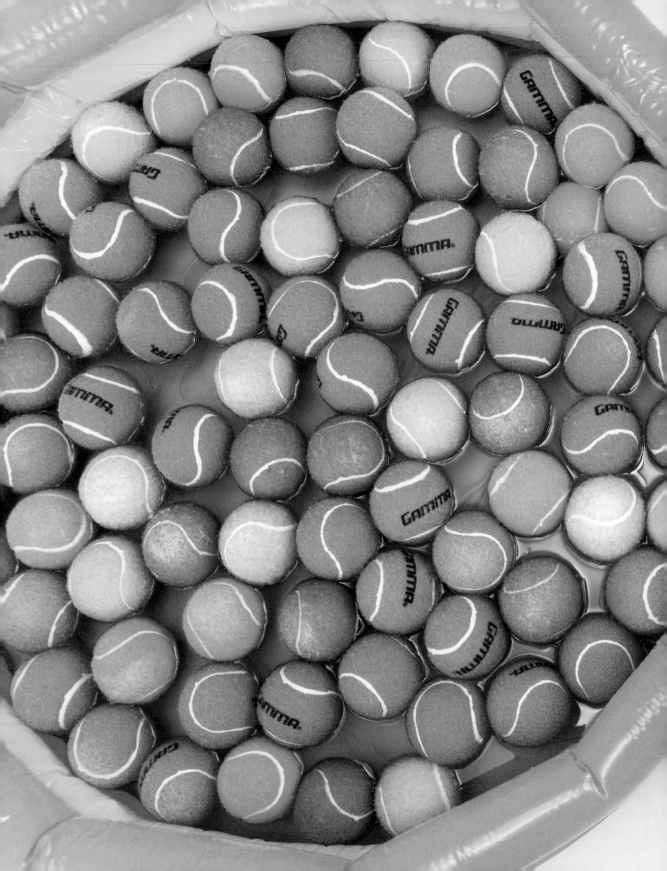

HOW TO THROW A PUPPY POOL PARTY

Is there anything better than a sunny day with your favorite people and pups? You don't need an in-ground swimming pool to host a dog-friendly backyard bash. Just grab a kiddie pool (or two!) and some snacks that work for both humans and dogs for a party that your guests will never forget.

No Party Poopers

For any pup party, having some poop bags available is a must.

Puppy Pool Party Ideas

Hang out in the sun, catch up with your friends, and visit with their dogs during this fun and easy backyard pool party.

🛡 Safety First

Before the party, make sure all the invited dogs are up on their vaccinations and that none of them have aggression issues or anxiety about being around other dogs. Also, many pups don't like water. You can still invite them, but don't force any into a situation that makes them unhappy. Carefully supervise the group of dogs at all times—both in the water and out of it.

Get Ready to Flamingle

A pack of lawn flamingos is a perfect easy decor option to set the mood. Some fun pool floats and inflatable beach balls are also great options.

Adult Swim

If you have the space, why not put out a kiddie pool for the humans, too? You can even float some balloons on the water for a 'gram-worthy background.

Twinning and Winning

Let your guests twin with their dogs by buying plain white cotton dog bandanas and scrunchies for the humans that they can tie-dye into matching sets. Because who doesn't want to match their dog?

Pool Off

When buying a pool for dogs, look for one with a durable bottom that can hold up against dog nails. Although there are dog-friendly pools available from pet retailers, in our experience, normal kids' pools work just as well for all but the very biggest pups. We love to float tennis balls in our dogs' pool for a fun surprise.

Just Add Water

Sure, the adventurous pups are probably happy to drink from the pool, but don't forget to set out a bowl of water for any dogs who are staying dry.

Save the Date

Use permanent marker to write your message on a mini pool float and drop it off at your guests' houses with their invite. Save yourself some stress by asking your guests to bring their own towel for their dog.

Dog-Friendly Fruit Kebabs

Fruit kebabs are one of those great treats that both humans and pups can enjoy. We love to use mini vegetable cutters on larger fruits like melon to create fun shapes. Just thread them on the skewer and you've got a treat that's almost too pretty to eat.

What to Do:

1. Use your small cookie cutters to create fun shapes from your selected fruits.
2. Thread the fruit onto a bamboo skewer for a treat that you and your dog can both enjoy—just remember to remove the skewer before serving to your pup.

❤ *Snack Safe*

The American Kennel Club's website is a great resource for learning more about which fruits and vegetables are considered safe for dogs. Always remember that some human favorites (like grapes) are poisonous to dogs.

✎ *Vet's Note*

Make sure that your pup isn't allowed to chew the bamboo skewer, as they can be dangerous if swallowed.

You'll Need:

- Dog-friendly fruit (strawberries, blueberries, cantaloupe, watermelon, apples, or pears)
- Small cookie cutters or vegetable cutters
- Bamboo skewers

Setting the Table for a Puppy Pool Party

Set the stage for your backyard bash with bright colors, mini pool floats, and treats that work for both pups and humans.

Cool Treats

Make tie-dye popsicles that your human and dog guests can share by alternating spoonfuls of blended dog-friendly fruit purees and plain yogurt into a popsicle mold.

Have a Ball

Tennis balls can double as decoration at outdoor pup parties. Not only are they a bright and cheerful design element, they'll also keep your four-legged guests busy and happy. But do be aware that tennis balls are not appropriate for all dogs, since some dogs chew so aggressively that they can damage their teeth or swallow part of the ball.

Float On

Don't forget to add some mini pool floats—they're adorable and they can work as drink holders for your human guests.

Made to Share

For a casual summer get-together, we love easy and refreshing snacks that work for both your human guests and pups. Use our Fruit Kebab recipe from p. 45 or simply offer your guests some freshly cut watermelon and summer berries.

AUTUMN

When the team at Tiller Press and I discussed writing this book, we knew that we wanted Halloween costumes to be a big part of it. Not only is it tough to find cute and inexpensive dog costumes, but many of the store-bought options are also uncomfortable for pups. While the Howloween picks here may not be the most elaborate options, they're fun and festive and the kind of costume that your dog might even fall asleep while wearing. (As Dave did over and over during our photo shoots.) And if costumes aren't your thing, we hope you enjoy some of our family's favorite pup-friendly fall recipes and other activity ideas for a memorable autumn.

Pupkin Spice Not-Latte

You'll Need:

- 1 used coffee cup sleeve
- 1 mini paper cup
- Hot glue gun
- Pumpkin sticker
- Handful of ice
- ½ cup plain and unsweetened canned pumpkin puree
- ⅛ cup of plain and unsweetened nonfat Greek yogurt
- Additional plain and unsweetened nonfat Greek yogurt for topping (optional)
- Cinnamon (optional)

We couldn't have a book about celebrating the seasons without including a pumpkin spice latte recipe, right? Here are step-by-step instructions for creating a sweet mini coffee cup for your dog, as well as a healthy pumpkin spice smoothie that they can enjoy.

What to Do:

1. Take a used coffee cup sleeve and trim it down to about 1 inch tall. Wrap it around a mini paper cup and glue into place. Add a pumpkin sticker for a little festive fun.
2. Blend the ice, pumpkin, and yogurt until smooth.
3. Pour a serving into a mini cup and top with a dollop of yogurt, if using. For the full effect, lightly sprinkle with cinnamon before serving.

Fall Scarf

Okay, I know: your dog doesn't really need a fall scarf. But will they look absolutely adorable wearing one? Yes, so case closed. I love using felt for DIYs like this because you don't have to do any sewing or hemming to keep it from fraying, plus it looks pretty darn cute as is.

What to Do:

1. Cut a long strip of felt for the scarf. For our dogs' scarves, I use a piece of felt that's roughly 30 inches by 6 inches.
2. Cut stripes and shapes out of your adhesive-backed felt and press onto the scarf. If you don't mind hot gluing, you can also use regular felt.
3. Trim along the sides of your scarf so that the edges line up perfectly. Cut into the ends of the scarf to create a fringe.
4. Give the scarf a quick pass with the iron to soften the stiffness of the adhesive-backed felt.
5. Optional: if you want the scarf to stay wrapped around your dog's neck in a specific way, glue a snap onto the scarf to hold it in place.

You'll Need:

- 2–3 feet felt in the color of your choice, adhesive-backed felt in other colors of your choice
- Hot glue gun (optional)
- Iron (optional)
- Snaps (optional)

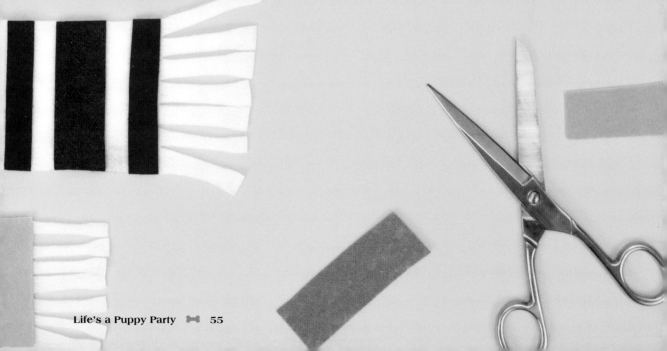

Witch Hat

You'll Need:

- 1 paper water cone
- 1 cardboard coaster
- Black spray paint
- Hot glue gun
- Spool of half-inch-wide elastic sewing band

My favorite kind of DIY is one that upcycles something that might be trash into a fun gift or costume. And this witch hat does that twice over! Combine an old cardboard coaster and a used paper water cone with a little black paint, and you've got yourself a mini witch hat!

What to Do:

1. In a well-ventilated area, spray-paint your water cone and a cardboard coaster black. You'll need to flip the coaster to paint its underside, too. After thoroughly spray-painting, allow to dry for 24 hours.
2. Once the paint has dried, hot glue the upside-down cone onto the coaster.
3. Eyeball how much sewing elastic you'll need to keep the witch hat on your dog's head. It should be just enough to attach to one side of the hat and then run down in front of your dog's ear, under their chin, and then back up to the other side of the hat in front of the other ear. It should be snug, but not tight. Glue the elastic into place on each side of the hat, and you've got an easy-peasy Howloween costume.

Woof in Sheep's Clothing Costume

Who else loves a punny Halloween costume? You can turn a plain black dog hoodie into a sheep costume in just a few simple steps. Plus, it's nice and cozy if you're taking your dog trick-or-treating on a cold October night.

What to Do:

1. Hot glue white poms all over the body of your dog hoodie. The number of poms you'll need will vary based on the size of your dog, but have enough on hand so that you can cover all of the hoodie other than the sleeves and the hood itself.

2. Cut two lemon-shaped ears out of the black felt and glue a small pink oval into the middle of each. Hot glue the ears onto each side of the hood.

3. Glue a googly eye to each side of the hood next to the ear.

You'll Need:

- 1 black dog hoodie in your dog's size
- Large white poms
- Hot glue gun
- Scissors
- 1 sheet of stiff black felt
- 1 sheet of pink felt
- 2 white googly eyes, 2 inches wide

Dogosaur Costume

You'll Need:

- 1 to 3 cardboard egg cartons (depending on the size of your dog)
- Scissors
- Dark green spray paint
- Hot glue gun
- 1 light green dog hoodie in your dog's size

Have you ever tried to DIY a Halloween costume and just had it be a complete failure? Me too. What I love about this one is that it's really, truly hard to goof up. I knew I wanted to include a dinosaur costume in the book because our one-year-old child is obsessed with them, but all the ideas I had involved a lot of sewing to make a ridge along the back of the costume that would stay standing up while our crazy dogs were wearing it.

While procrastinating instead of sewing, I was staring into the refrigerator, thinking about making scrambled eggs but also thinking about making a dinosaur costume, and it suddenly occurred to me that the egg carton was the perfect shape to be a spiky dinosaur ridge. I spray-painted it and glued it to a hoodie, and it has become one of my favorite DIYs in this book. Not only is it incredibly easy, but your dogs will hardly know they're wearing a costume.

What to Do:

1. Take a cardboard carton for a dozen eggs. Trim off the lid and discard. Then trim away all of the lower carton except the spikes running down the center that separate the two rows of egg cups. Depending on the size of your dog, you might need more than one carton; you'll want enough spikes to run the length of your pup's back. For instance, for Dave we used one, but for Lizzie we used two.
2. Spray paint the outside of the spikes dark green and allow to dry for 24 hours.
3. Hot glue the spikes in a line along the back of the hoodie.

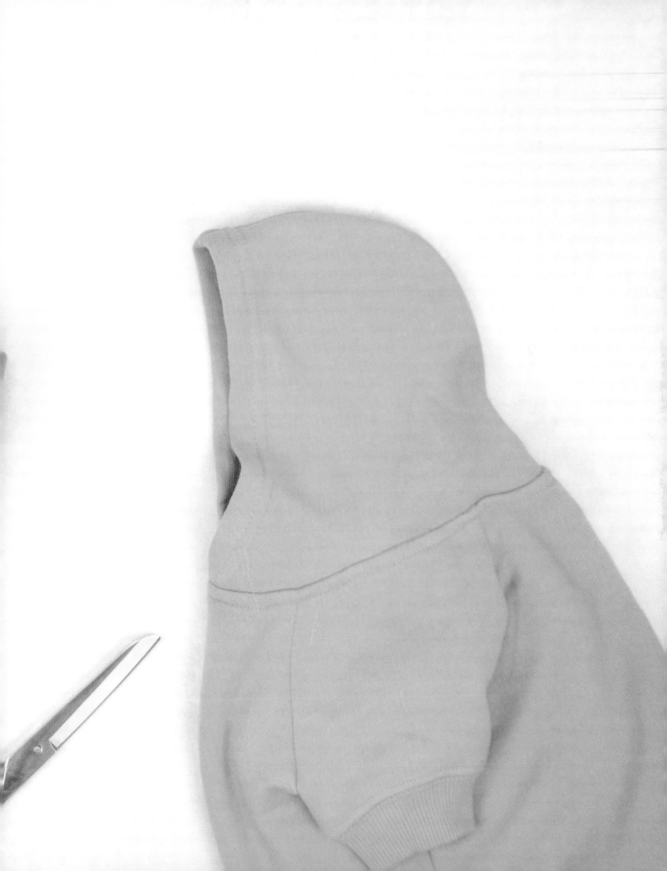

Two-Ingredient Ghost Pops

Makes 4 ghost pops.

When I was seven, I was invited to my first-ever Halloween party. We were each asked to bring a homemade treat, and my mom helped me make a version of these pops using a recipe from a magazine—little white-chocolate Halloween ghosts with red cinnamon-candy eyes. Everyone at the party loved the ghosts, and I was so proud that I remember requesting ghosty lollipops for the next few months. Since they'll always have a special place in my heart, I wanted to create a version for the dogs. Not only is it an adorable fall treat, it also might be the easiest recipe in this book.

You'll Need:

- 4 popsicle sticks
- 1 cup plain and unsweetened nonfat Greek yogurt
- 4 blackberries

What to Do:

1. Line a baking sheet with wax paper and place the popsicle sticks on it.
2. Stir the yogurt until smooth and then glob it on top of the popsicle sticks in little ghosty shapes. Give them eyes with little round pieces of blackberries.
3. Place the baking sheet in the freezer for 2 hours.
4. Hold on to the popsicle stick and allow your pup to lick away at the spooky treat!

🐾 Don't forget that popsicle treats should be shared while you're holding on to the stick so your dog doesn't accidentally ingest the wood.

Who's ready for

Howloween?

Unicorn Costume

I think we can all agree that unicorns have been having a moment the past few years, so I was surprised when I went looking for a unicorn Halloween costume for our dogs' last Halloween and couldn't find anything I liked. Everything was too tacky, too pricey, or too uncomfortable for the dogs. I decided to make my own costume and it was way easier than I imagined. Not only do I love how this one turned out, it's actually surprisingly easy to pull together.

What to Do:

1. Save a used paper water cone and coat the outside of it with Mod Podge using a paintbrush. Roll the cone in glitter and allow it to dry until it has set completely. Then add another coat of Mod Podge to seal the glitter.
2. When the glittery cone is completely dry, wrap three loops of washi tape around it to create a spiral unicorn horn effect. If your washi tape isn't sticking to the glitter on its own, hot glue it into place. This is your unicorn horn.
3. Hot glue the horn onto the top of the sweatshirt hood.
4. Cut your yarn into around 100 15-inch strands. (For a bigger dog, you'll need more.)
5. Run glue down the center of the back of the hood and press the middle of each strand into the glue so that the strand extends to each side, forming a mane. Allow to cool completely, and then comb the two sides into the center to form the unicorn mane. Trim away any odd pieces.
6. Give the unicorn ears by cutting two lemon-shaped pieces from the white felt and gluing a pink oval inside. Glue the ears onto each side of the hood.
7. Zip your dog into the hoodie and just like that, pure magic.

You'll Need:

- 1 paper water cone
- Mod Podge
- Paintbrush
- Clear glitter
- Glitter washi tape
- Hot glue gun
- 1 white dog hoodie in your dog's size
- 1 ball of pastel yarn (an ombre or multicolored yarn works best)
- 1 sheet of stiff white felt
- 1 sheet of pink felt

Wheat-Free Autumn
Apple Dog Treats

You'll Need:

- 1½ cups oats
- 1 large apple
- ¼ cup coconut oil, melted
- ¼ cup coconut flour
- Cookie cutters

Makes 12 biscuits.

Lots of families have a pecan pie or pumpkin pie tradition in the fall, but my family is definitely an apple pie family. So for me, apple pie always smells like coming home for the holidays. Even though the sweet and decadent apple pie my family loves is off limits for our pups, I think these treats are the next best thing. The coconut oil gives them a rich buttery flavor, while the apple makes them smell like fall. Not only are they Dave's favorite biscuits in this book, they're also wheat-free, dairy-free, and egg-free, which makes them perfect for pups with sensitive stomachs.

What to Do:

1. Preheat oven to 325°F and line a baking sheet with parchment paper.
2. In a food processor, blend the oats until they are thoroughly ground.
3. Remove the apple's core and discard. Then add the rest of the apple to the blender with the oats. Blend until the apple and the oats form a coarse and sticky dough. If your apple is too dry to mix well with the oats, add a teaspoon of water.
4. Remove the dough from the blender and place in a medium bowl. Mix in the coconut oil and coconut flour.
5. Roll out the dough on a surface lightly dusted with coconut flour until it's about ¼ inch thick. Use a small cookie cutter to punch out shapes and place them on the prepared baking sheet.
6. Bake for 20 minutes and allow to cool on the baking sheet.

HOW TO THROW
A HARRY PAWTER
PARTY

I know that Harry Potter isn't exclusively set in the fall, but something about the changing weather just makes me want to curl up with a cup of tea and a cinnamon candle and reread *The Prisoner of Azkaban.*

Lizzie's birthday is October 8, so when I sat down to plan her first birthday celebration, all I could think about was how much I really wanted to create a Harry Potter–themed party for dogs. So we did! We went all out on making Dogwarts decor and cooking up a storm of magical treats. We posted the pictures on our blog, and it's still one of our most read posts two years later. I think it might even be my favorite party I've ever thrown—for a dog or a human!

Since so many of our readers loved the post, we recreated it for this book, complete with some new easy recipes and updated DIYs. So, whether you're celebrating a barkday party, a Gotcha Day, or just the fall season, I hope you have a magical get-together with these tips and tricks.

Harry Pawter Party Ideas

Welcome your furry guests to Dogwarts with these fun and easy ideas for a magical bash.

Lumos! Set the tone for your pup party with battery-powered candles. You can make it look like they're floating by hot gluing thread to them and taping the other end of the thread to the ceiling.

Buy an inexpensive plastic cauldron and fill it with dog biscuits for a themed treat.

Use the Pumpkin Spice Not-Latte recipe on p. 50 and put it in a mini beer glass for an easy, dog-friendly Butterbeer.

Serve Not-Chocolate Frogs by following the instructions for the Not-Chocolate Easter Bunny (p. 19) and swapping the rabbit mold for a frog mold to create this magical treat.

Send your party invites by owl! Tape your invite to a plush owl dog toy and drop it off at your guests' homes. Almost as good as Hedwig, right?

Need to make your party invites and signage look old and magical? Soak them in tea and then let them dry before you use them.

Is your pup a Ravenpaw or a Hufflepup? Invite your guests to make scarves in their dogs' house colors using the DIY on page 55.

Favor Bags for a Harry Pawter Party

Keep the magic going by sending your guests home with a cute bag of themed, pup-friendly party favors.

Gift your guests their own lightning bolt cookie cutter and a recipe for making Lightning Bolt Biscuits (p. 85) at home.

Use the Witch Hat DIY on p. 56 as a magical party favor for your guests.

Send your guests home with the scarves they made at the party—they'll be perfect to reuse for Halloween costumes.

A bully stick looks almost like a wand, right?

Find pup-sized fake glasses by browsing the children's section of costume stores.

Lightning Bolt Biscuits

Makes 8 to 10 biscuits.

These lightning bolt treats are a great addition to any Harry Pawter party spread or favor bag. Not only are they easy to make but our pups are completely obsessed with them. You can use the recipe for any type of shape, but they work especially well as lightning bolts since the pumpkin naturally gives the dough a yellow tint.

What to Do:

1. Preheat oven to 350°F and line a baking sheet with parchment paper.
2. Whisk together the flour and baking soda, and then stir in the pumpkin and coconut oil.
3. Roll out the dough until it is roughly ¼-inch thick. Punch out lightning bolts using your cookie cutter.
4. Bake for 10 to 12 minutes and cool on rack.

You'll Need:

- 1 cup whole wheat flour
- ½ teaspoon baking soda
- ¼ cup plain unsweetened pumpkin puree
- ¼ cup coconut oil, melted

WINTER

❄

Anyone else have a secret soft spot for the cold winter months? I love the cozy weather and the excuse to stay home with our pups. Whether you're looking for giftable DIYs, an advent calendar, or special holiday treats, we've got ideas for how you can celebrate the season with your dog.

Dog-Toy Advent Calendar

I am a complete sucker for advent calendars, which I blame on my incredibly creative mother who sewed us an elaborate advent calendar when we were kids. Even though I'm not nearly as crafty as she is—and definitely not as patient!—you don't need any creative-genius skills to make this adorable dog-toy holiday countdown. Not only does it double as a tabletop decoration, but our dogs also get incredibly excited about playing with a new toy each day of the holiday season.

What to Do:

1. Label 24 tennis balls with glitter numbers from 1 through 24.
2. Hang the tennis balls on the Christmas tree by running a hanging hook through the fuzz of the ball—one for each day of the holiday season.
3. Take down one ball each day, remove its hook and number, and then give it to your dog to enjoy!

♥ Stay Safe

Don't risk your dog sneaking one of the tennis balls off the tree and eating a hook. Keep the advent calendar out of your pup's reach, and be especially cautious if you have a larger dog who can reach tabletop spaces. Additionally, be aware that tennis balls are not appropriate for all dogs, since some dogs chew so aggressively that they can damage their teeth or swallow part of the ball.

You'll Need:

- 24 tennis balls in the color of your choice
- Glitter sticker numbers 1 through 24
- Small tabletop Christmas tree
- 24 ornament hanging hooks

Easy Ugly Holiday Sweater

You'll Need:

- Decorations of your choice including iron-on patches, poms, pearls, embroidery thread, or puff paint
- 1 knit dog sweater in your dog's size
- Hot glue gun

When planning an ugly sweater party a few years ago, I noticed how hard it was to find some fabulously tacky and silly holiday sweaters for our dogs. The only ones I could find cost way more money than I was willing to spend on a goofy clothing item. This easy hack makes an ugly sweater that looks just as good as a store-bought one and is maybe even more fun. I mean, look at those dinosaurs!

What to Do:

1. Browse craft stores and online retailers for the most festive and tacky iron-on holiday patches you can find.
2. Use a hot glue gun to deck out your sweater in true tacky fabulousness.

Who says dinosaurs aren't festive?

Holiday Gift Jar
and Star Dog Treats

You'll Need:

- ½ cup creamy all-natural and xylitol-free peanut butter
- 1 cup whole wheat flour
- ½ cup plain unsweetened applesauce
- Mini star cookie cutter (or any festive shape!)
- 2 8-ounce Mason jars with clamp lids
- Baker's twine
- Star tinsel wire
- 1 kraft paper gift tag

Makes 2 Mason jars full of treats.

Homemade gifts are the perfect way to show how much you care while still sticking to your budget during the expensive holiday season. This is one of our all-time favorite recipes for an easy dog treat, and wrapping them up in a Mason jar decked in starry tinsel wire and baker's twine elevates it to a thoughtful and Pinterest-worthy present.

What to Do:

1. Preheat oven to 350°F and line a baking sheet with parchment paper.
2. In a small bowl, mix the peanut butter, flour, and applesauce.
3. Roll out the dough on a lightly floured surface until it's roughly ¼-inch thick. Punch out shapes using a mini cookie cutter and place on the prepared baking sheet.
4. Bake for 10 minutes and then allow to cool on a cooling rack.
5. When the treats have cooled completely, place them in the mini Mason jars. Wrap with twine and star wire, and then add a gift tag for the lucky recipient.

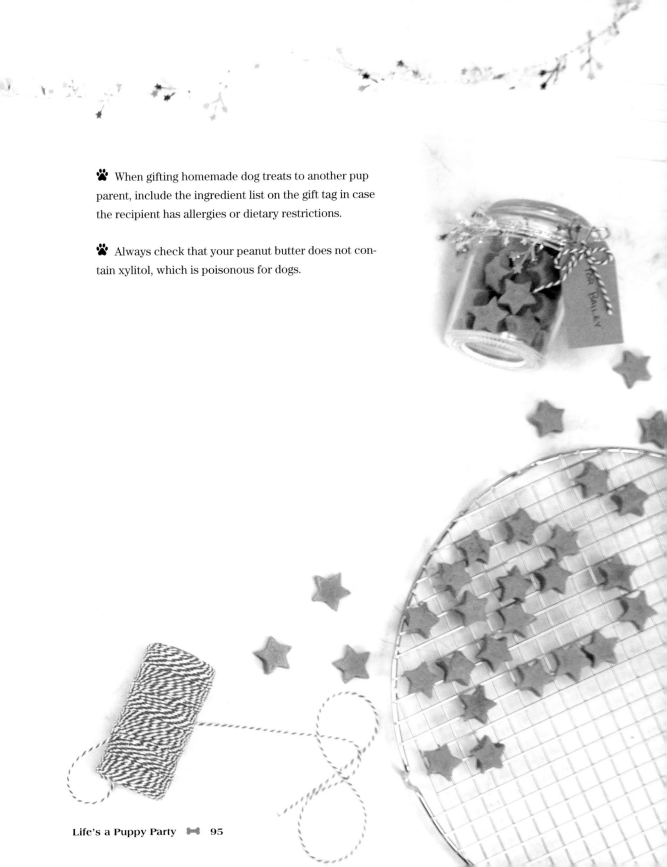

When gifting homemade dog treats to another pup parent, include the ingredient list on the gift tag in case the recipient has allergies or dietary restrictions.

Always check that your peanut butter does not contain xylitol, which is poisonous for dogs.

Holiday Wreath Chew Toy

You'll Need:

- Green fleece
- 1 rope or rubber chewing ring
- 1 sheet of pink or red felt

When we first brought Dave home, I went all out buying him beautiful plush dog toys. And he destroyed every one of them in minutes. Literally minutes. I had no idea that such a small dog would be able to decimate toys that were twice his size so quickly and efficiently. Because of his sharp little teeth, sewing him a toy isn't really an option, which is why I love this festive holiday wreath toy. Not only does it combine the excitement of a snuffle mat with the fun of a chew toy, it's also easy to make and our dogs still haven't figured out how to destroy it. Does it get better than that?

What to Do:

1. Cut the green fleece into 12-inch strips. Double knot the strips onto the chewing ring, leaving 2 to 3 inches of fleece strip hanging off each side of the knot.
2. Knot your way around the ring until it's completely covered. This is your wreath. Trim away any odd ends so that the wreath looks consistent.
3. Cut a small rectangle and a thin strip of felt. Use the strip to tie the rectangle onto the wreath so that it looks like a bow. Give to your dog to enjoy!

✎ Vet's Note

Please be aware that this toy is not appropriate for dogs who have a tendency to ingest cloth toys, as swallowing cloth can cause bowel obstructions.

Pawfect Holiday Ornament

Who says kids are the only ones who get to create salt dough Christmas ornaments? Make an ornament showcasing your pup's paw that you'll cherish for years to come.

What to Do:

1. Preheat oven to 275°F. Line a baking sheet with parchment paper.
2. In a small bowl, mix together the flour, salt, and water until it forms a moldable dough. Roll dough flat until it's roughly half an inch thick.
3. Smear coconut oil across your dog's paw to protect it from the salt. Gently press your dog's paw onto the dough so it leaves a print behind. Wipe their paw clean.
4. Center the paw print under a water glass and then punch it out to create your ornament. Carefully move it to your lined baking sheet.
5. Use a toothpick to create a small hole at the top of the ornament for your ribbon.
6. Bake for 3 hours and then remove from oven. Allow to cool completely.
7. Spray paint your ornament white and then allow to dry completely.
8. Once the paint is dry, coat all of the ornament except the paw print with Mod Podge and dip in clear glitter. Allow to dry, then add another coat of Mod Podge to seal the glitter in place.
9. Add a ribbon and hang on your tree!

You'll Need:

- 1 cup flour
- ½ cup salt
- ½ cup water
- 1 tablespoon coconut oil
- 1 round water glass
- 1 toothpick
- White spray paint
- Mod Podge
- Glitter
- 7-inch piece of ribbon

✏ Vet's Note

Make sure that you hang this and any other salt dough ornaments on your tree well out of reach of your dog, since ingesting it could potentially lead to salt toxicity.

New Year's Black *and* White Push-Pop Treats

You'll Need:

- 1 cup whole wheat flour
- ½ teaspoon baking soda
- ½ teaspoon baking powder
- 2 eggs
- ⅓ cup coconut oil, melted
- ¾ cup unsweetened carob chips
- 2 cups plain and unsweetened nonfat Greek yogurt
- 2 packets plain unsweetened xylitol-free gelatin
- 1 piping bag
- 4 plastic push-pop containers
- New Year's stickers (optional)

Makes 4 push pops.

I love making confetti push pops for just about every occasion, so I knew I wanted to develop a festive push-pop treat for the New Year. These special black-and-white pops are the perfect way to ring in the New Year with your pup. Layer dog-friendly "brownies" with healthy yogurt for a treat that might even make your dog forget about all the fireworks outside.

What to Do:

1. Preheat oven to 350°F and spray an 8 x 8-inch pan with nonstick cooking spray.
2. In a medium bowl, whisk together the flour, baking soda, and baking powder. Stir in the eggs and melted coconut oil.
3. In a small glass bowl, heat the carob chips in the microwave. Pause and stir in 10-second increments until the chips are completely melted. Mix the melted carob chips into the medium bowl to create your brownie mixture.
4. Spread the brownie mixture across the bottom of the prepared pan and bake for 20 minutes. Remove from the oven and allow the brownies to cool completely before using.
5. Meanwhile, mix the yogurt and gelatin together and place the mixture in a piping bag. Set aside.
6. Prepare your push pops by washing the containers thoroughly and then decorating them with the stickers of your choice.
7. Crumble the cooled brownies and begin to fill the push-pop containers, alternating layers of brownie with the piped yogurt mixture. Top with a swirl of yogurt and a crumble of brownies, or one of the Star Dog Treats from page 94.
8. Keep refrigerated until you're ready to serve.

:paw: Don't forget, push pops should always be served to dogs while held by a human. Don't ever leave your dog to eat out of a push pop unsupervised as they could eat the plastic.

✏ Vet's Note

As mentioned before, monitor the introduction of carob into your dog's diet, and always check ingredient lists to make sure the gelatin and yogurt you're using are free of xylitol.

New Year's Eve Dog Bow Tie

Got New Year's plans that require bark-tie attire? No one will guess that you crafted this glam bow tie yourself—and without a stitch of sewing! Plus, it's so lightweight and easy that your dog might not even notice they're wearing it.

What to Do:

1. Cut a 3-by-5-inch rectangle of black felt, as well as a ½-by-5-inch strip of black felt.

2. Using puff paint, create rows of gold glitter dots across your felt rectangle. Allow to dry completely.

3. To create a bow, accordion-fold your felt rectangle lengthwise and then pinch the felt in the center of the fold. Hot glue one end of your felt strip to the top of the pinch. Wrap the rest of the strip around the bow and then glue into place with just enough excess strip left to create a loop that fits snugly around your dog's collar. Glue that loop into place so the bow tie can slide on and off the collar.

4. Thread your dog's collar through the loop and they'll be ready to party 'til midnight!

You'll Need:

- 1 5-inch-by-5-inch square stiff black felt
- Gold glitter puff paint
- Hot glue gun
- 1 dog collar

Valentine's Day Box of Not-Chocolate Strawberry Bites

You'll Need:

- 2 cups oats
- 1 cup fresh strawberries, with stems removed
- 1 teaspoon coconut oil, melted, plus additional drops
- ¼ cup coconut flour
- ⅓ cup unsweetened carob chips

Makes 25 bites.

Anyone else agree that chocolate is the best part of Valentine's Day? Even though chocolate is a huge no-no for dogs, these strawberry "truffles" are almost as good. You start with a nutritious strawberry oat base that gets a fab glow up with a little drizzle of melted carob chips. Plus, they're wheat-free, which is handy for pups with sensitivities. Wrap them up in a heart-shaped box for a perfect finish!

What to Do:

1. Preheat oven to 350°F.
2. In a blender, puree the oats and strawberries until they form a sticky dough. Remove from the blender and place in a medium bowl.
3. Stir in the coconut oil and coconut flour.
4. Line a baking sheet with parchment paper. Roll the mixture into tablespoon-sized balls and place on the lined sheet.
5. Bake on the oven's middle rack for 10 minutes. Remove from the oven and leave the oat balls on the pan to cool.
6. Once the oat balls have cooled completely, place carob chips in a glass bowl and microwave. Pause and stir the carob every 10 seconds to keep it from burning.
7. Once the carob is fully melted, stir in a few drops of liquid coconut oil to make the mixture truly runny.
8. Place the melted carob into a plastic bag and snip off the very tip of the corner. While the oat balls are still on the parchment paper–lined sheet, drizzle with the carob and allow to set.
9. For a little extra pizzazz, place your finished treats in mini muffin papers and place in a heart-shaped box!

Bee Mine
Valentine's Day Costume

Looking for a cute Valentine's Day outfit for your dog? Why not show the world that the two of you bee-long together! This no-fuss costume is pretty darn adorable, and it comes together in a pinch. Just don't forget to take a picture.

What to Do:

1. Cut two round wings out of the cardstock and hot glue them to the dog tee near the back of the neck. Set aside.
2. Measure how much sewing elastic you'll need for your dog's headband by running the elastic under their chin and over the top of their head in front of their ears. You'll want enough elastic so that the band will be snug, but not uncomfortably tight. When you've taken your measurement, add an extra half inch of elastic and then cut. Use the extra half inch to overlap the ends of the elastic and hot glue them together to make the band into a loop. Set aside.
3. Take the black pipe cleaners and glue a medium black pom to the tip of each. These will be the bee antennae. Trim off roughly half of each pipe cleaner to keep the length manageable.
4. Take one of the bee antennae and wrap the pom-free end around the elastic loop. Twist it around several times until it's tightly attached to the headband. Secure the second antenna the same way, about two inches from the first. If your headband is too loose, the antennae won't stay in place, so make sure it's fitted to your dog.
5. Painter's tape doesn't have any stretch, so put your dog in their tee before adding the tape. Once they're wearing the tee, add two strips of tape wrapped around the belly of the shirt. Just be careful to avoid catching any of your pup's hair in the tape!
6. Take a pic with your bee-utiful Valentine!

You'll Need:

- 2 sheets white cardstock
- Hot glue gun
- 1 black dog tee in your dog's size
- Spool of half-inch-wide elastic sewing band
- 2 black pipe cleaners
- 2 medium black poms
- Yellow painter's tape

 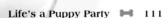

St. Patrick's Day Leprechaun Costume

You'll Need:

- Green spray paint
- Small paper cup
- 1 cardboard coaster
- Hot glue gun
- 1 sheet of black felt, cut into thin strips
- 1 sheet of gold glitter paper
- Spool of half-inch-wide elastic sewing band
- 1 sheet of dark green felt
- 1 green tee in your dog's size

Get your dog in on the fun of St. Paddy's Day with this cute and easy leprechaun—ahem, pup-rechaun—costume. The best part? You can create the hat by reusing a paper cup and a cardboard coaster. Whether your pup's Irish or not, everyone's definitely going to want to give them some St. Patrick's Day kisses.

What to Do:

1. In a well-ventilated area, spray-paint the outside of a small paper cup and both sides of the cardboard coaster green. Depending on your paint, you may need to apply a second coat. After thoroughly spray painting, allow to dry for 24 hours.

2. Once the paint has dried, hot glue the upside-down cup onto the coaster.

3. Wrap a thin strip of black felt around the top lip of the cup and cut a small square frame of gold paper for the hat buckle. Hot glue both into place.

4. Eyeball how much sewing elastic you'll need to keep the leprechaun hat on your dog's head. It should be just enough to attach to one side of the hat and then run down in front of your dog's ear, under their chin, and then back up to the other side of the hat in front of the other ear. It should be snug, but not tight. Glue the elastic into place on each side of the hat.

5. For the body of the leprechaun costume, accordion fold a rectangle of green felt and then pinch the center to form a bow tie. Hot glue a thin strip of felt around the pinched portion to hold it in place and then hot glue the bow tie on to the neck of the green tee.

6. Add a belt to the costume by gluing another thin strip of black felt and another square of gold paper for the belt buckle to the middle of the tee.

Anyone else get almost as excited about their dog's birthday as their own? I know that our dogs probably/definitely don't know that their birthdays are different than any other day, but I still love going all out to spoil them once a year. (Or twice a year—half birthdays are a thing in our house!) Even if my pups aren't keeping track of their barkdays, they absolutely appreciate getting showered with extra love and attention. Seeing them jump for joy and wag their little tails always melts my heart.

When you're planning your pup's barkday party, the most important thing to remember is that it should be fun for both you and your dog. While Lizzie is a classic corgi and loves playing with other dogs and meeting new people, Dave is a stereotypical dachshund and would prefer to just spend time with his group of five or so people that he already knows and loves. To accommodate all types of dogs, I've intentionally included activities and recipes in this section that work for groups of any size—whether you're celebrating with a whole bunch of friends and their dogs or flying solo with your own canine pal.

And remember, if you adopted a dog and don't know their birthday, all of these ideas will work for a Gotcha Day party, too. Because the day they joined your family is definitely worth celebrating!

Now go get the confetti and the pupcakes, because in dog years, it's time to party!

Bake *the* Perfect Pink Pupcake

You'll Need for the Sweet Potato Pupcakes:

- 1½ cups whole wheat flour
- 1 teaspoon baking powder
- ¾ cups canned unsweetened sweet potato puree
- ½ cup coconut oil
- ⅓ cup plain and unsweetened nonfat Greek yogurt
- 1 egg

You'll Need for the Frosting:

- 2 cups plain and unsweetened nonfat Greek yogurt
- 2 packets unflavored unsweetened xylitol-free gelatin
- 1 teaspoon natural beet juice

Makes 6 pupcakes.

I've spent a long time trying to bake the perfect barkday pupcake. Creating a dog-friendly cake isn't too tricky, but frosting? That's another story. All of the dog frosting I'd previously found in recipes online was made with ingredients I didn't really want to feed our dogs, or it was ugly and runny. My dream was to develop a healthy frosting that could be put in a piping bag to make a perfect—and Instagrammable!—cupcake swirl that our dogs would love.

After trying approximately a bajillion different combinations, on a whim I added some plain gelatin to Greek yogurt. Not only are both ingredients good for dogs, but the gelatin thickens and smooths the yogurt so that it's just right for piping onto a cupcake—pretty similar to a classic cream cheese frosting. Just add a splash of beet juice, and you've got yourself perfect pink pupcake frosting!

Of course, the best part is that our dogs absolutely love this recipe, and I feel good knowing that they're getting a bunch of healthy ingredients. Win-win!

What to Do:

1. Preheat oven to 350°F. Set out baking cups or prepare a muffin pan with wrappers or all-natural nonstick cooking spray.
2. In a medium bowl, whisk together the flour and baking powder. Set aside.
3. In a large bowl, mix together the sweet potato puree, coconut oil, yogurt, and egg.
4. Stir the dry ingredients into the wet ingredients, mixing thoroughly.
5. Fill cupcake cups with batter until they are roughly ¾ full.
6. Bake for 20 to 25 minutes. Remove and allow to cool completely before frosting.

7. In a large mixing bowl, combine the yogurt and gelatin. Mix thoroughly. Yogurt texture can vary, so if your yogurt is runny, sprinkle in some extra gelatin until the consistency is similar to a classic cream cheese frosting.

8. Once you've thoroughly mixed in the gelatin, stir in the beet juice for color.

9. I like to use a piping bag, but you can frost your pupcakes using any method of your choice. Since you're working with yogurt, don't frost your cupcakes until shortly before serving, and keep them refrigerated between frosting and serving.

♥ Safety First

If you choose to use candles, keep them far away from your dog. You don't want to risk your pup trying to sneak a taste of the dessert and getting burned.

✎ Vet's Note

Always check ingredient lists to make sure you're using plain and unsweetened yogurt and gelatin, since many of the flavored and sweetened varieties contain xylitol, which is toxic for dogs. Additionally, be sure to remove cupcake wrappers before feeding pupcakes to your dog.

Happy Barkday!

How to Make a Puppy Party Hat

Next time you're at the gym, don't throw your paper water cone away—take it home and turn it into a party hat for your dog! You can even make yourself one to match. How you decorate is up to you, but stickers, washi tape, puff paint, or glitter are all great options. Top your hat with a pom, and it's officially time to party!

What to Do:

1. Outside or in a well-ventilated area, spray-paint the outside of your water cone. Allow the paint to fully dry for around 24 hours.
2. Decorate your cone with stickers, puff paint, glitter, pictures, washi tape, or other craft supplies. Glue the pom to the tip of the cone.
3. Eyeball how much sewing elastic you'll need to keep the party hat on your dog's head. It should be just enough to attach to one side of the hat and then run down in front of your dog's ear, under their chin, and then back up to the other side of the hat in front of the other ear. It should be snug, but not tight. Glue the elastic into place on each side of the hat.
4. Have fun partying with your pup!

! Share the Fun

If you're throwing a birthday bash, invite your guests to decorate their dogs' own party hats. Just prep by spray-painting some paper cones ahead of time and set out your decorating materials, a hot glue gun, and a spool of elastic band for guests to use.

You'll Need:

- 1 paper water cone
- Spray paint in the color of your choice
- Decorations such as stickers, puff paint, glitter, cut-out pictures of your dog, or washi tape
- Hot glue gun
- 1 small pom
- Spool of half-inch-wide elastic sewing band

Planning Your
Pup's Barkday Party

You know your dog better than anyone, so when you're planning their birthday bash, take their personal preferences and needs into account. Here are some fun ideas to get you started.

Chews Your Own Adventure

Nothing gets party guests chatting and mingling like some shared activities. One fun and easy DIY that works for dogs of all sizes is to offer your guests materials for making a rope toy. Look for rope in bright, naturally dyed colors, and then invite your guests to knot or braid a toy their dog will love.

Puppy Love

Is there any better decoration than your dog's adorable face? Find a photo of your dog against a neutral and un-cluttered background and print multiple copies of it. Cut out your pup and use the photos for party decorations—for everything from wall decor to garlands to invites. After all, it's your dog's party!

Stay Cool

In our household, it's not a real party without ice cream. Brands like The Bear & The Rat, Bazzy's Kefir, and Swell Gelato all make delicious (and adorable!) frozen treats for dogs that are easy to serve at any gathering.

Gift Better

Instead of your guests bringing barkday gifts, consider asking them to donate to a rescue organization. A few of our favorites are Little Paws Dachshund Rescue, Second Chance Rescue, and Old Friends Senior Dog Sanctuary.

Safety First

Any time you get a group of dogs together, it's important to put safety first. Make sure all the invited dogs are up on their vaccinations and that none of them have aggression issues or anxiety about being around other dogs. After all, your pup party should be fun for everyone!

Just Add Water

Always set out a water bowl to keep your furry guests hydrated!

Dogs Will Be Dogs

Don't forget to have poop bags available!

Building the Perfect
Barkday Party Favor Bag

Keep the puppy party going by sending your guests home with some of this cute loot.

You can never have too many poop bags, especially cute and biodegradable ones like these. Throw a cute sticker onto the roll to keep it wound tight.

Treats are always a good idea!

Most pups can never have too many rope toys. Plus, they make festive and inexpensive party favors.

Personalize a generic gift bag by pasting a cut-out picture of your pup's adorable face onto the front.

Pup parents at your party will thank you for these adventure-ready pop-out water bowls.

Setting Your
Barkday Party Table

Just because your four-legged guests won't be sitting at the table doesn't mean it can't look cute.

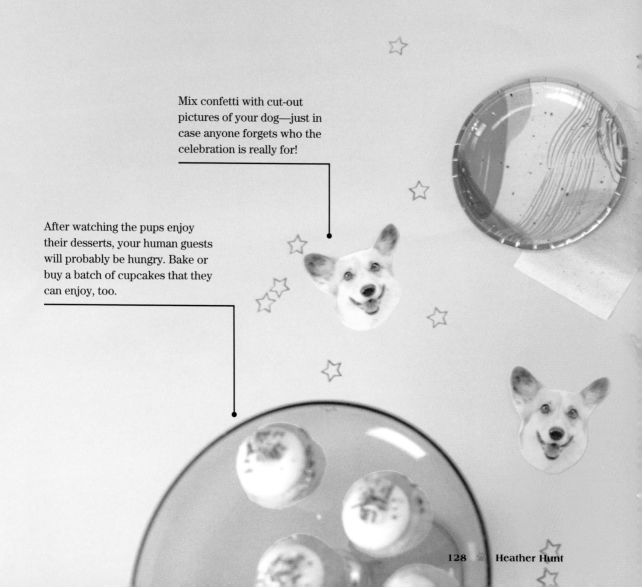

Mix confetti with cut-out pictures of your dog—just in case anyone forgets who the celebration is really for!

After watching the pups enjoy their desserts, your human guests will probably be hungry. Bake or buy a batch of cupcakes that they can enjoy, too.

Top your pupcakes with small dog biscuits to make sure your human guests don't accidentally snack on the pup treats!

Dog biscuits are a great no-mess party treat. Buy them at the store or bake them using one of the recipes in this book.

Sprinkles Barkday Bandana

Confession: sometimes I put sprinkles on my morning oatmeal. Why? Because sprinkles just make everything happier. And even though the real deal is off limits for dogs, this no-sew bandana is the perfect way to make any old day feel like a party. Whether you decide to incorporate this DIY as a barkday party activity or make one of these as a Gotcha Day gift, you're sure to brighten someone's day with this fun pattern. But no promises that you won't be craving a sprinkles doughnut by the time you're done.

What to Do:

1. Fold the felt square diagonally and glue the ribbon inside, along the fold. Leave about 5 inches of ribbon on each side, so you can tie the bandana around your dog's neck. You may need more or less than 10 inches depending on the size of your dog.
2. Cut the scraps of pastel felt into small rectangles roughly 1 x ¼ inches. Glue into place on the felt square in a random pattern.
3. To smooth your design, give it a quick pass with the iron when you're done gluing.

You'll Need:

- 1 square of white or light pink felt, approximately 10 inches
- 1 ribbon, approximately 20 inches long
- Hot glue gun
- Scraps of pastel felt
- Iron (optional)

Barkday Party Photo Booth

You'll Need:

- 20 to 40 large dog biscuits
- Pastel spray paint in the colors of your choice
- 1 trifold poster board
- Hot glue gun
- Sticky Putty (optional)

Capture gorgeous photo-booth-style pics of all the four-legged guests at your pup's barkday with this easy DIY that uses a good old trifold poster board and a big box of dog biscuits. Just make sure that your hungry guests don't eat the backdrop!

What to Do:

1. Outdoors or in a well-ventilated area, lay the dog biscuits on newspaper and spray-paint them. Depending on your brand of spray paint, your biscuits may need more than one coat of paint. Allow the paint to fully dry for around 24 hours.
2. Using your hot glue gun, glue biscuits to the front of the trifold poster board in a random pattern.
3. You don't need a professional lighting set for your photos to look great, but make sure that you set up the poster board somewhere that has natural light, avoiding direct sunlight or shadows.

💡 Go Big

If you're trying to capture a pic of dogs who are too big to fit in front of poster board, it can be easier to use a white wall with good natural lighting as a backdrop. Just swap the hot glue for some Sticky Putty and decorate the wall for your photo background instead. And as an added bonus, it'll give you space to set the camera timer and get in on the fun!

MORE RESOURCES

As much as I love crafting DIYs and baking for our dogs, sometimes I just want to buy a gift, toy, or treat for them. After years of blogging about the best places to shop for pups, I have more than a few favorite brands that always deliver gorgeous products. We've pulled together a list of our favorites to make shopping a little easier for you.

WHERE WE SHOP

When Dave first joined our family, one of my biggest surprises was how hard it was to find high-quality and design-oriented dog gear and accessories. But through the growth of our wonderful online community, I was introduced to an incredible network of talented small business owners and inspiring entrepreneurs who revolutionized how I shop for our dogs. I'm so excited to get to share some of my favorite places to buy treats, party supplies, and beautiful gifts for dogs and dog lovers.

Our Favorite Places to Buy Party Treats for Dogs

Want to treat your dog, but skip the time in the kitchen? Some of our favorite small businesses for dog owners create healthy and delicious treats for dogs.

Bazzy's Kefir
bazzyskefir.com

Spotted Dog Bakery
spotteddogbakery.com

The Bear & The Rat
cooltreatsfordogs.com

Seattle Barkery
theseattlebarkery.com

Portland Pet Food Company
portlandpetfoodcompany.com

Bubba Rose Biscuit Co.
bubbarose.com

Whisk & Wag
whiskandwagtreats.com

Bocce's Bakery
boccesbakery.com

Swell Gelato
swellgelato.com

Wufers
wufers.com

Our Favorite Small Businesses for Buying Dog Gifts

Looking for the perfect barkday gift for your pup or their BFF? These are our absolute favorite places to shop for beautiful and well-made pup products both large and small.

Dapper Dexter
dapperdexter.com

All the Best Pet Care
allthebestpetcare.com

Boris & Horton
borisandhorton.com

Fable
fablepets.com

Bumble & Hound
bumbleandhound.com

Dash & Co.
shopdashandco.com

Dog & Co.
shopdogandco.com

Florence & Ottie
florenceandottie.com

Delightful Dapple
delightfuldapple.com

Fluff & Tuff
fluffandtuff.com

Finn + Me
finnandme.com

Favor
infavorof.com

Haute Dawg
hautedawgshop.com

KindTail
kindtail.com

Gift Spawt
giftspawt.com

Get Wagging
getwagging.com

Hunter & June
hunterandjune.co

Love Thy Beast
lovethybeast.com

Milo & Me
shopmiloandme.com

MODERNBEAST
modernbeast.com

Love Harlso
harlso.com

PUPSTYLE
pupstylestore.com

Rebel Dawg
rebeldawg.com

Pablo & Co.
pabloandco.net

Ripley & Rue
ripleyandrue.com

R'n'D Paws
rndpaws.com

Sassy Woof
sassywoof.com

Sir Dogwood
sirdogwood.com

Waggo
waggo.com

Trill Paws
trillpaws.com

The Foggy Dog
thefoggydog.com

Wagwear
wagwear.com

Wild One
wildone.com

Whiskers & Stitched
etsy.com/shop/WhiskersandStitched

Woof & Wonder
woofandwonder.com

Zoomies
zoomiesnyc.com

Zozo's Paw
zozospaw.com

Our Favorite Places to Buy Puppy Party Supplies

Whether we're planning a barkday blowout or just looking for a few small touches to make a get-together extra memorable, we love to source our party supplies from the gorgeous goods at these shops.

Buster's Party Shop
etsy.com/shop/BustersPartyShop

Daydream Society
daydreamsociety.com

Meri Meri
merimeri.com

Paper Source
papersource.co

Mylle
inflatable pools
mylleshop.com

My Sticker Face
mystickerface.com

Our Favorite Places to Buy Feel-Good Gifts for Dog Lovers

We love giving (and getting!) gifts that help pups in need. Here are a few of our favorite places to shop for dog-lover gifts that give back.

Grounds & Hounds Coffee Co.
groundsandhoundscoffee.com

Pearls for Pups Co.
pearlsforpupsco.org

Rescue Me Candle Company
etsy.com/shop/rescuemecandleco

Rescue Dog Wines
rescuedogwines.com

Scripted Fragrance
scriptedfragrance.com

SOURCES *in this* BOOK'S PHOTOS

ACKNOWLEDGMENTS

I couldn't be more grateful for the many, many people (and dogs!) who made this book possible.

First of all, working with the team at Tiller Press has been an absolute dream. A big thank-you to Michael Anderson and Ronnie Alvarado for persuading me to write this book with their enthusiasm and passion for the project. Ronnie was truly the most wonderful guiding editor and definitely deserves a vacation after months of graciously fielding my anxious emails. Huge thanks to Patrick Sullivan, Matt Ryan, and Jenny Chung for turning a big Dropbox of dog photos into a gorgeous book. I knew that I was going to love working with Laura Flavin as soon as she told me about her dorgi obsession, and I'm so grateful to her, Lauren Ollerhead, and Molly Pieper for getting the word out about this book. Special thanks to Megan Gerrity and Benjamin Holmes. Most important, thank you to Theresa DiMasi for believing in this book.

I feel so incredibly lucky to have connected with Dr. Sarah Machell through the serendipity of the internet. It has truly been a joy to work with someone so knowledgeable and kind. Thank you for all your time and care to review this book and make sure it was safe for pups.

My parents have an amazing gift for materializing when I need them, and they showed up over and over to babysit and cheer me on during this crazy year. Writing a book in a pandemic with a job and a busy toddler was more challenging than I ever imagined, and I couldn't have done it without them. B is the luckiest kid to have you both in her life. And Dad, thanks for letting me name my dachshund after you. I'm sorry that everyone now calls you "Human Dave."

Before I created The Dapple, I always thought the internet was all bots and bullies, but I have met some of the loveliest people I've ever known through Instagram and our blog—probably because dog people are the best. You all know who you are, and I'm so grateful for each and every one of you who have been cheering on our little blog from the beginning. Thank you to our loyal readers, our small business partners, everyone who has participated in our holiday magazines, the friends in the Peace & Love Insta chat, and all the people who take the time to message or comment on our posts. It really means the world.

Finally, this book would never have been written without the most important person in my life, my kind and funny husband, Josh. Not only did he manage to somehow turn our basement playroom into a pandemic-proof photo studio and shoot thousands of dog photos for this book, he kept me laughing and sane through the most stressful moments of this crazy year. Thank you for all the coffee runs, bok choy dinners, and tropical house playlists.

INDEX

ABOUT *the* AUTHOR

Heather Hunt is an obsessed pup parent and the founder of the lifestyle site TheDapple.com, which she launched in November 2017 after struggling to find modern dog products, travel recommendations, and activities for her dachshund, Dave. Heather lives in Seattle with her husband, daughter, and two spoiled dogs, Dave the Dachshund and Elizabeth the Corgi. Their home is very full of joy and dog hair.